GUILDFORD PAST AND PRESENT

BY PHILIP HUTCHINSON

This book is dedicated to Eddie and Sarah
— the best two friends I ever had.

ACKNOWLEDGEMENTS

I would like to offer my thanks to Simon Moulden, Peter Williams, Chris Quinn, Martin Leech and Jennifer Haynes for providing some of the old images in the book. Thanks too to Peter Sillick, Simon Harvey-Williams and Alice Fage for taking (and the permission to use) some of the more striking modern photographs. Also, I wish to acknowledge the assistance of Zandra Boodhoo and her staff at Bateman's Opticians, Richard Christophers and the staff of the Surrey Archaeological Society, Mary Alexander and Carol Brown. Lastly, I want to extend my debt to David Rose, Stanley Newman, John Janaway, Matthew Alexander and the late Mark Sturley and Russell Chamberlain for writing books on Guildford history that were so useful to my research.

First published 2009

The History Press
The Mill, Brimscombe Port
Stroud, Gloucestershire, GL5 2QG
www.thehistorypress.co.uk

© Philip Hutchinson, 2009

The right of Philip Hutchinson to be identified as the Author of this work has been asserted in accordance with the Copyrights, Designs and Patents Act 1988.

British Library Cataloguing in Publication Data.
A catalogue record for this book is available from the British Library.

ISBN 978 0 7524 5127 5

Typesetting and origination by The History Press
Printed in Great Britain

CONTENTS

An unknown delivery boy, making his rounds in an unknown Guildford street. This damaged 'tintype' photograph, badly faded and printed back to front, came from a collection of Guildford photographs. Research to discover the location has so far remained fruitless, although it gives an impression of the Woodbridge Road area. There is a small chance the young man sitting in front of all that bread is James Gwinn, whose family had been running a bakery in Chapel Street since 1832. If the identification were correct, this photo would date to *c.* 1925. The bakery has closed but the building still stands. It may also be one of the delivery boys for the Hine Bakery, which was at 19 Woodbridge Road.

INTRODUCTION

Guildford's topography is rather like the face of someone you know well. If you see them every day, you won't notice the signs of ageing. If you don't see them for years, the changes are all too apparent. As someone who lives in Guildford and loves the town (in spite of its rather unlovable faults), it rarely fails to surprise me when I meet an ex-resident whose first words tend to be 'Hasn't it changed?', or 'I hardly recognise the place'.

Putting this book together has shown me that those people who remember a halcyon Guildford are more often than not quite right. I tend to blank out the ugly and utilitarian modern structures in the town – and who wouldn't? I only see the Victorian gables, the warped rooflines, the 1868 setts running up the steep High Street and that classic protruding clock on the Guildhall, the third most photographed timepiece in England. On a sunny day, on a winter's morning or even in a downpour, looking towards The Mount whilst standing in front of the Guildhall makes me feel alive. It also makes me feel those who have trod upon the street in antiquity are also still here in some way.

I can say this in the knowledge that this is not a unique or even particularly eccentric opinion. Guildford has many individuals and several organisations that love its heritage just as much – and in some cases considerably more – than I do. I'm not a Guildfordian by birth; though I've worked in the town since 1994 (running the Castle Keep), I only moved here from Hampshire and started the popular ghost tours in 2001. But it's home, and I could not imagine moving anywhere else.

Living in Guildford, and the knowledge that I live here, never fails to thrill me. I am proud of what Guildford was and what it struggles to be, though I have a profound dislike of what it turns into in certain areas after dark and even walk a longer route home from Guildford Station on Friday and Saturday nights to avoid them. I am glad it is a side of Guildford that tourists do not see and console myself it is a part-time modern malaise affecting almost every town in the country.

However, before I go off into a rant more suited to the age and politics of someone entirely different, I should comment that I cannot think of any other place within easily commutable distance from London that captures the quintessential English market-town so well as Guildford. It is because of this that, in spite of having limited attractions, the town plays host to masses of tourists every year.

I could open my own museum with the amount of Guildford ephemera I've accumulated over the years. I have boxes of artefacts, album upon album of postcards and photographs and shelves full of books. Few things excite me as much as finding a unique snapshot of Guildford in a shoebox at a postcard fair. Maybe I need to get out more often. Much to the annoyance of other collectors, I rarely see a Guildford item on eBay that I don't have without mercilessly chasing it. Having accrued such a cornucopia, I don't like to see history swallowed up – I like to share it (some would say boast about it). As the collection is always growing, consequently this is my third Guildford-related book for The History Press.

I love publications full of comparative images. Even if you don't know the places shown, they are always intriguing. My issue here was using pictures that had not been seen before. I could easily have filled another book with images I had intended to use that I then noticed had been published already by other local authors (particularly grating when I'd spent a small fortune on purchasing the image in the first place). I have to come clean and confess there are probably about a dozen images in here you might have seen before, but there have been reasons why I've chosen to include them; either the matching modern image was of greater relevance, or the older image had been used some years ago in books now out of print.

I should also maybe apologise to people expecting to see images of the outlying area. There were so many shots I could have used I decided to concentrate almost solely on the town centre, or places within ten minutes walk. Not only does this bring focus to the book, but it also meant I very rarely had to make troublesome journeys. In fact, the one part of the book I had not been looking forward to was stepping out in the depths of winter to make comparative shots, yet this is actually the aspect of the work I have enjoyed above all others.

One thing my publisher had warned me about was the difficulty in getting modern shots to match the standards of the old ones. Clearly, early lenses were able to show a nice, straight elevation of a building and my little camera (although I am fond of its results) doesn't have that capability. Also, modern Guildford may frequently look dull and drab here. It's not. Winter meant less leaves on the trees to block the views and the lack of sun meant that I could take photographs of buildings without too many obscuring shadows cast over them. The sun actually shines on Guildford like everywhere else.

Every image in this book has gone through PhotoShop software. In the case of the modern images, it has been to crop them to the same dimensions as the old ones. For the older images, all had to undergo a degree of restoration. This includes the removal of text at the bottom of postcards, taking out spots and creases and – in the case of the 1906 image of Josephs Road – a huge amount of work from a folded, torn, faded and foxed unique albumen photograph that had cost me £5 in one of those postcard fair shoe boxes.

Dividing the book into chapters was not an easy task and in the end I had to opt for a general division of locale, with specialist themes at the end. Because of my connection to Guildford Castle, I make no apologies for setting aside a whole chapter for images of its environs. I could have made a whole book from my castle collection alone.

I hope you will find these comparative photographs interesting. I also hope that in twenty years time you can pick up this book and not find that some of the 'now' photographs have become 'then' photographs!

Philip Hutchinson,
Guildford,
June 2009

1

THE HIGH STREET AND
NORTH STREET

The High Street from the town bridge, *c.* 1925. This was taken from far further down than you might think. The last complete building on the left still stands, albeit right next to Millbrook today. At this time, it served as Cawdron's draper's store. Cawdron's suffered a great deal of damage and loss of stock in the floods of 1928. Just visible on the extreme left is part of the Bridge House Hotel, which shut shortly after this was taken and was demolished in 1971. The building closest to the photographer on the right was the last one before you crossed the bridge.

The position of the old Cawdron's store shows just how far the buildings once extended. Today, you have to stand a long way back even from the later main road to get the same angle. Although the southern stretch of Millbrook was built in 1961, the part leading from the Friary did not open until 1973, and so for a decade traffic still had to pass along Friary Street, turn right and then sharp left into the main route.

Looking down the High Street towards the town bridge just before the First World War. At that time, long before Millbrook was constructed, houses reached right down to the bridge on both sides.

As happens so often in Guildford, one side of the street remains fairly unaltered whilst the other has been swept away. Although the bottom of the right-hand side was lost in the Millbrook extension of the 1970s, the remaining structures on that side are intact. Until 2008, there was a subway crossing underneath Millbrook. Long redundant, this has now been filled in and no evidence remains. The author was the last member of the public to be permitted access and was given a tile from the extensive wall mural as a keepsake.

The image here post-dates 1950, when the pinnacle on the roof of St Nicolas' (it lost the 'h' in the 1880s) church was removed. It is also prior to 1956, when the Lion Hotel (originally The White Lion) shut its doors that September to be demolished for the construction of Woolworth. The decorations thus date it to the coronation celebrations of Queen Elizabeth II in 1953. The expansive White's store is on the right. The High Street pleasingly flows right over the town bridge towards The Mount as it had done since ancient times.

The old building on the left remains unscathed. The pavement has been widened considerably at the junction with Quarry Street to allow the main area of the High Street with setts on the road to be gated during shop hours, allowing pedestrians to roam freely. Although there are nods to old styles of architecture, most of the old buildings visible in the previous image have gone and have been replaced by the dull right angles of the late twentieth century.

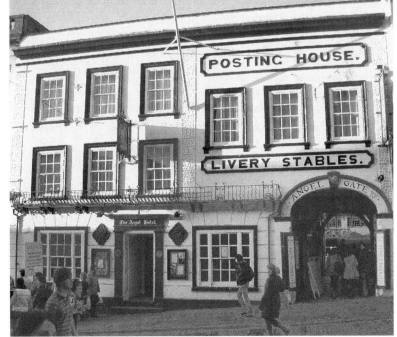

Thought to take its name from the angel that once surmounted the ancient Fish Cross outside, the Angel is the final remaining coaching inn in Guildford. The motorist in this photograph, taken *c.* 1920, may be hinting at the fact the building served at this time as an HQ for the Automobile Association.

Beloved of tourists and those with deep pockets, the Angel was almost forced to close in 1989 but just pulled itself back from the brink to being a highly respected establishment, whose front elevation never fails to charm the passer-by as a reminder of days now gone. It appears to no longer be a family hotel however!

Looking past the Angel Hotel up the High Street in a view by Drewetts, the prolific stationer and local photographer, in the 1890s.

Although the ground-level shop fronts have changed, if you look up you will see very few differences between the two views. This is one section of Guildford that has managed to resist too much modernisation, and looks all the better for it.

Tunsgate Arch and the Tudor houses adjoining it *c.* 1920. The arch was the portico for the corn market from 1818 to 1901, when the buildings behind were demolished and the market moved to Woodbridge Road. A fire damaged the two nearest gabled buildings on the right on New Year's Day in 1922. Although the two buildings were destroyed, no one was injured. Behind the group of men in the middle is the entrance to Smallpiece's Gateway, one of the many tiny alleys Guildford possessed at the time. The only remaining example today with any semblance of the original character is Milkhouse Gate nearby.

The central pillars of the arch were moved eight feet apart at the end of 1936 to give road access. The road no longer runs under the archway, which is now set with a large mosaic in its floor commemorating the twinning of Guildford with Freiburg in Germany. The fire-damaged houses were rebuilt in exactly the same fashion, although Smallpiece's Gateway disappeared forever at the same time. External renovation work to the building closest to the arch exposed the original wattle and daub construction in 2006.

Looking down the High Street in the late 1880s. The current Guildhall dates from *c.* 1550, although it has much earlier foundations. The clock mechanism came a decade later and John Aylward's famous projecting clock face is from 1683. The clock face was actually replaced in the Victorian years, the one with which we are familiar being reinstated in 1898. According to the late historian Russell Chamberlain, the story concerning Aylward making a gift of the clock in return for the right to trade in the town may be local folklore. The building next to the Guildhall on our side was put up in 1884. Note the smashing tricycle in front of Jeffrey's sports shop on the left.

The buildings on either side of the road closest to the photographer have new frontages and the pavement widens underneath the Guildhall, but otherwise little has altered in the foreground. You can still feel the old charm of this part of the High Street.

Looking up the High Street in the mid-1860s, before setts were put down in the road. Prominent in this image is Haydon's Bank founded by the draper William Haydon in 1765. In the distance can just be seen two of the turrets of Abbot's Hospital, founded by George Abbot in 1619. The gatehouse was modelled on that of Hampton Court Palace.

Remarkably, almost everything has survived. The bank (at that point renamed the Capital & Counties) was extended in 1899 and the shop front to its left was lost. It was the first case of local pressure in Guildford actually saving a building from destruction, for the old bank was earmarked to be replaced. It has been home to Lloyd's Bank since 1920. The interior of the building is still highly impressive.

155 High Street (now better known as Guildford House and once numbered 25) was built by John Child in 1660 and is one of the most architecturally prized buildings in the town. It served as a family home until it became various shops between 1844 and 1928. We see it here in the 1890s, when it was serving as Bull's sports shop.

Bought by the Guildford Corporation in 1957, Guildford House is now the home of the town's main art gallery. Virtually nothing has changed over the years and the renovation work that has taken place has generally been to restore rather than replace.

This view looking along Upper High Street from Ram Corner in the early 1900s was printed in Berlin. Before the First World War, a lot of postcards came from Germany as they had some of the best printing presses.

Most of the right-hand side of the street remains, although greatly disfigured by modern shop fronts. Nothing whatsoever is left of the other side of the road. It was all razed to the ground in the 1960s and the road was widened.

Looking down towards The Royal Grammar School on the Upper High Street. The current building, colloquially known as 'Old School', was started in the 1550s, taking several decades to be built from brick and Horsham stone. This scene was captured in the mid-1880s and shows how much drabber this architectural gem would be without the whitewash we see today.

A fire on 2 December 1962 severely damaged parts of the building, although the esteemed chained library was saved. No longer the main part of the school, it is still used for some classes. Note that one pair of windows on the top left was unblocked shortly after the previous image was taken.

The Duke of Somerset had Somerset House built to accommodate him when travelling between London and his main seat at Petworth. He had the impressive structure placed just outside the parish boundary to prevent having to pay dues to the town. Here, we see it around 1920, though it remained unaltered for centuries.

Plans have been submitted in an attempt to somehow restore the aesthetic appeal of Somerset House by making the awful shop fronts more harmonious with the surroundings, but these have been overlooked and Somerset House is today hiding behind a truly ugly mask.

A picture of the White Horse Hotel in the early 1940s from a billhead of 1945. The hotel has its origins in the eighteenth century and sits at the top of the High Street at the junctions of London and Epsom Road. At this time, the managers were Mr & Mrs J W Morris. A double room, according to the bill, cost £1 a night.

The White Horse, retaining the large statue above the doorway, is now the Guildford Hotel. Although it appears to be unchanged, the interior and rear section were mostly demolished and rebuilt to modern specifications in 1964 and it was again refurbished in 1988.

A view down the top of North Street in 1948. The late Victorian extension to Cloth Hall on the extreme left was home to Clark's College. The old fire station building and the Horse & Groom pub can be seen on the bend of the road. Filling the right-hand side of the image is Pimms furniture store. These buildings were pulled down in the 1960s.

Do not be fooled by a single car! The author had to dash into the middle of the road between streams of traffic to snap this. North Street is extremely busy and always full of vehicles. As elsewhere in Guildford, the hanging light spanning the road has gone. The old Pimms buildings were replaced in the late 1960s by this soulless structure. Amongst other duties, it houses TGI Fridays and the 96.4 Eagle radio station.

Opposite above: The Royal Arms Temperance Hotel in North Street as it looked *c.* 1920. It was built under the instruction of the Revd Paynter from nearby Stoke church in 1881 to encourage a teetotal lifestyle at a time when the movement was gaining a lot of popularity.

Opposite below: As with many old Guildford buildings, a lick of paint has done wonders. The only thing that has disappeared from the earlier view is the large plaque on the roof. The Royal Bank of Scotland uses the ground floor and the upper floors have been home for many years to The Guildford Institute, who took up tenancy only a decade after the building was erected.

Right: Market Street looking south from North Street, *c.* 1910. The building on the left was designed by the prolific Guildford architect Henry Peak and was erected in 1895. It spent many years as the home of Gammons Ltd, a local clothier. They traded here until the 1960s. Market Street itself was once the yard of the Red Lion Inn, which was on the High Street side of Market Street, furthest from the Guildhall. Charles II is rumoured to have stayed there and Samuel Pepys certainly did. (Image courtesy of Chris Quinn)

Market Street is to some extent a forgotten gem in Guildford, largely used as the primary thoroughfare between the two main shopping roads. However, it once held the popular Guildford Theatre and many of the old buildings still exist if you look above the bland modern shop fronts. Although Friary Street, Swan Lane, Angel Gate and Jeffries Passage all link the High Street to North Street, this is the only one still possessing any pretensions of being a proper street rather than a pedestrian walkway.

North Street in the 1900s. Instantly recognisable in books, completely unrecognisable on site today. North Street was originally the site of the Medieval town ditch and went by the insalubrious name of Lower Back Side in the eighteenth century. The impressive Methodist church of 1899 dominates the view. On the right, Henry Peak's charming Post Office building. A tree so far from the pavement in North Street today would be extremely out of place!

Initially, North Street looks unrecognisable, but if you compare the less significant buildings you will see that quite a lot do actually survive. The Post Office, however, was replaced in 1972 and the church torn down a year later. Needless to say, their replacements have no merit. The Post Office moved to the top of North Street in 2006 and much of the right-hand side of the road is under threat of demolition because of plans to extend the Friary Centre.

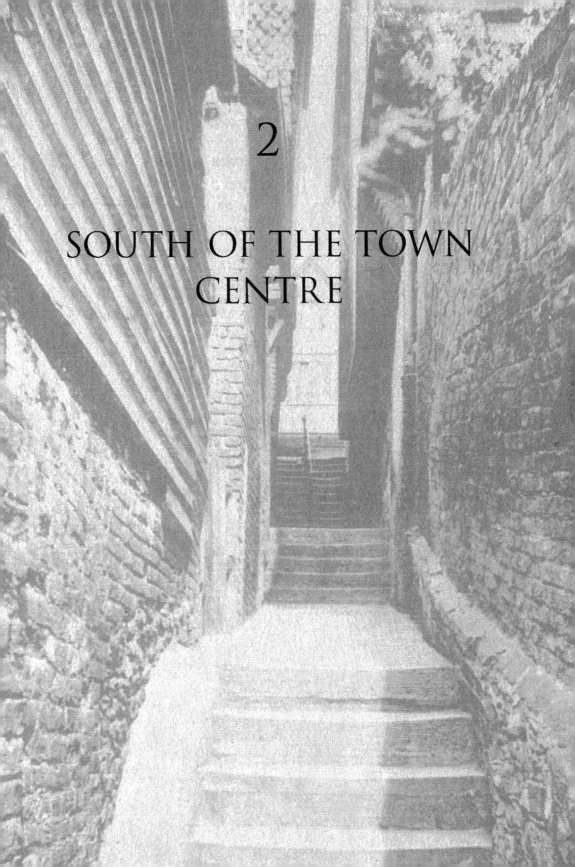

2

SOUTH OF THE TOWN CENTRE

Houses at the top of Castle Hill, shortly after construction in the 1860s. The author Lewis Carroll rented The Chestnuts (built 1861) at the bottom of this road for his six spinster sisters in 1868. He would spend breaks in Guildford and after catching pneumonia whilst walking over the nearby hills at Christmas 1897, he died in the house on 14 January 1898 and is buried in The Mount cemetery.

Remarkably, all that has been lost in 150 years is sections of wall to make car-parking spaces. The houses have survived without any apparent alteration. Castle Hill is still difficult for vehicles to negotiate and accidents are not unheard of. A few years ago, one vehicle went right through the wall at the bottom of the hill leading into Castle Cliffe Gardens.

The chalk caverns in Racks Close as they looked at the time they were opened for the first organised public tours in 1930. The caverns are Medieval in origin and have no links with the many myths that have grown up around them over the years. They were almost certainly nothing more than quarries for the local clunch chalk and do not connect to anywhere else. The caverns were open twice a week throughout the 1930s but tours stopped with the outbreak of war. Deemed unsafe, they were sealed for good in the 1950s.

A composite of three shots taken through tiny holes in the grille of the new gate leading into the caverns' entrance in January 2008. It was the first time the caverns had been accessed for quarter of a century. Prior to this, they lay buried deep under the soil. At this stage, a new concrete base with access hatch was placed above the old entrance to make future access more straightforward. The caverns must be checked periodically to ensure they are sound and to release the accumulation of gases. This view of the entrance shows exactly why there will be no more public access.

Quarry Street looking down towards the High Street in the early 1900s. At the bend in the distance was once Guildford's House of Correction, remnants of which were discovered in recent renovations. The church is St Mary's. It is believed that Guildford originally grew around this site in the early Saxon period. Although the crenallations at the top are more recent, the tower is known to be the oldest standing building is Guildford and dates to before the Norman Invasion.

Old-fashioned lenses make the modern view look like the church has shrunk and moved further down the street. Just off to the right, one building front has been demolished. The old trees in the churchyard have been removed and replaced. The pavement has actually been widened in the foreground (partially to better guide vehicles into the very narrow and sharp turning up Castle Street). Otherwise, things are as they always were.

This may look like a Victorian slum, but this is in fact Castle Street, close to the junction with Quarry Street, as it looked in 1970. It was around this time that a large part of Castle Street, particularly that on the side adjoining the castle itself, was being ripped down. Although they appear to be unlikely candidates, these buildings were saved.

Whitewashed and looking far grander today, the buildings have undergone a transformation. Most notable is the walkway made through one of the houses to a small area giving access to the back of a restaurant, a photographer's, offices and the side door to Salter's, run as a Victorian schoolroom by Guildford Museum.

Rosemary Alley, linking Millbrook to Quarry Street, as it appeared in the early 1900s. The alley originally possessed a less salubrious title, plainly stating its primary purpose at that time as little more than an open sewage drain. The ancient buildings still stand, cosmetically unaltered, at the Quarry Street end. On the left you can see part of the wall of the pumping station designed by the Guildford architect Henry Peak. It was demolished in the 1950s during the massive road building scheme. At the time this was taken, however, Rosemary Alley didn't lead out to the busy Shalford Road and Yvonne Arnaud Theatre as it does today. Millbrook was once a cul-de-sac, ending at The Mill itself.

The same spot today and looking virtually unaltered. The only major change has been the widening of this middle and lower part of the alley. When a building was erected on the site of the former pumping station (which itself served as a mortuary from 1904), it did not extend so far to the south, giving some extra inches of space for people negotiating the steps. The replacement building is used as a rehearsal space for the Guildford Conservatoire (formerly the Guildford School of Acting). Rosemary Alley may provide a short cut, but many will testify to their regret when reaching Quarry Street because the steps become steeper the higher you ascend.

A beautifully composed (posed?) shot of boys fishing at Millmead in the early 1900s. Most of them are on a small pontoon of what appear to be sandbags, jutting out into the shallow waters. In the distance, the tower of St Nicolas' church can just be discerned.

The bridge remains but the boys have long gone, already having lived and died. The river is now deeper at this point and the banks have eroded, so the group would have been largely underwater today. The bridge leads from the car park and Council Offices at Millmead, past the side of the Yvonne Arnaud Theatre, and onto Millbrook, leading up to the town centre.

Millmead in the 1900s, looking across the River Wey towards St Mary's church on the left and the Town Mill to its immediate right. The small cluster of buildings around it belonged to an iron foundry that was demolished in 1941. In the middle distance are the backs of the houses in Quarry Street. At that time, they all had long, steeply sloping gardens that were eventually lost when Millbrook was built.

Willow trees on the island in the river next to the lock partially obscure the Yvonne Arnaud Theatre, named after the actress and pianist who lived in London Road and died in 1958. The theatre was opened in 1965 and is one of the most highly regarded in the country, hosting many plays before they transfer to the larger London theatres. The single-storey buildings on the right survived the purge. Directly above them you can just make out the brooding silhouette of the Castle Keep, a couple of hundred yards uphill.

Tumbling Bay, a weir just outside the town centre linking part of the Wey Navigation with the River Wey itself, as it looked *c.* 1905.

At this spot, although there is a pair of 1960s high-rise blocks on The Mount, nothing has been developed. The tree coverage is less on the far bank and others have grown on the pontoons between the weir. Much of the bank on the other side of Tumbling Bay has eroded and been replaced with a modern revetment, but the structure itself is unaltered.

This charming house, well-hidden but situated next to The Jolly Farmer (or, more recently, The Weyside) pub, was not – as this 1920s postcard would have you believe – constructed in 1403. It dates instead to *c.* 1600, although there may be elements of the building older than this. To have taken this picture, the photographer would have been standing in a place impossible to reach today, as there are now steep steps leading down to the house.

Still standing in 2009 – but for how much longer? Thankfully, applications to have the building demolished have been flatly refused and the owner has since considered having it physically removed and erected elsewhere. Although undoubtedly a house of great charm, it is entirely at the mercy of the River Wey and has seriously flooded over the years.

Looking along Quarry Street from the fringes of Guildford, *c.* 1920. This was the main road out of Guildford in the direction of Shalford and Horsham and always meant that traffic had to pass along the very narrow town centre end of Quarry Street. In 1810, part of the chancel of St Mary's church was demolished to widen the road. If that part of the church had remained, it would have been no wider than an alleyway.

Millbrook was opened for traffic in February 1962. It meant that nearly all the houses on the southern side of Quarry Street, regardless of age or pedigree, were demolished. Quarry Street now sees far less traffic and the main A281 road cuts right through the site of the gardens that belonged to the lost houses.

The Jolly Farmer pub has its origins in the mid-nineteenth century. The main building was part of a collection of cottages, a shop, a wheelwright's and a blacksmith's. This is the original pub, seen *c*. 1900 from the river. The boathouses of Charles Leroy, so familiar on old picture postcards of Guildford, flank the pub and a wonderful dog can just be seen lying close to the back door.

This view may well be unique in that a total rebuilding of the site has actually made it more picturesque. The replacement pub from 1913 has far greater architectural merit than its predecessor. Now called The Weyside, it is a popular watering hole not only for Guildfordians, but also for people using the river. Although some are still dotted about, note that none of the buildings from the first image are visible here.

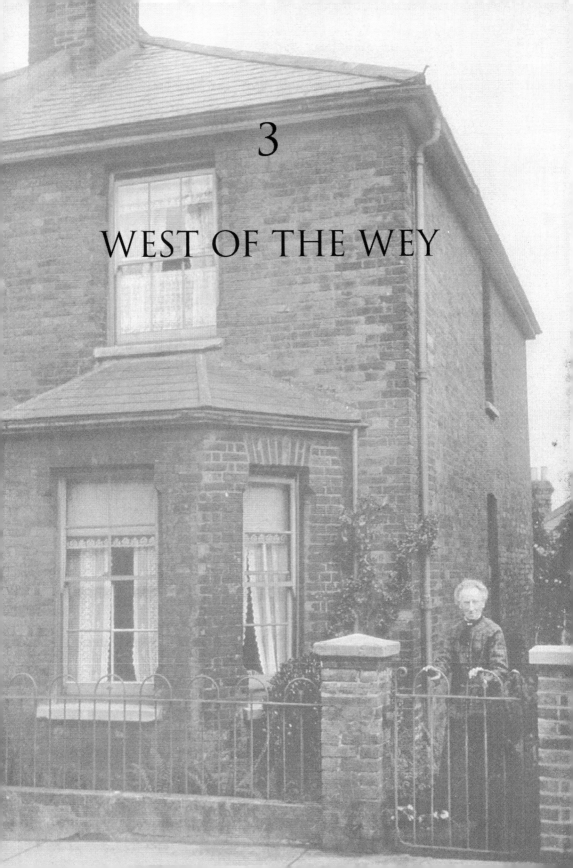

3

WEST OF THE WEY

A scene that will bring back memories to many people. Shot from the first floor of the building serving as The White House pub, this is the Farnham Road bus station in the 1950s. It had been opened in the 1940s following the demolition of the Connaught Hotel. There was a second bus station in nearby Onslow Street. That bus station is where the forecourt of the Electric Theatre lies today.

Yet again, at a loss with what to do with the area, the site of the old bus station is yet another unkempt car park. To the right of the pub on the left is the birthplace of George Abbot. The pub was known for many years as the Greyhound, but is now, more suitably, eponymously named after James I's Archbishop of Canterbury.

The second church of St Nicholas, built by Robert Ebbels in 1837 and retaining the tower of the original Medieval church. The building had been partially constructed with sub-standard concrete and was always dark and damp. When cracks started showing in the walls, it was decided to rebuild it again. This rare image from the bottom of Mount Street was taken in the mid-1860s. To the right is the shop of Robert Stone, the stationer and picture-framer.

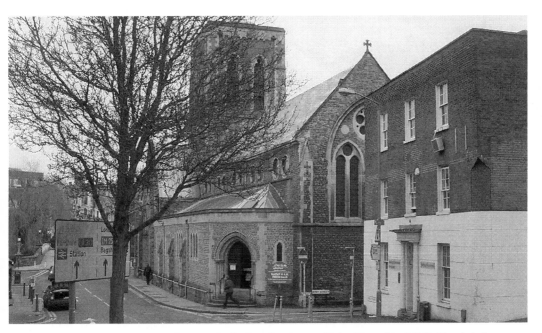

St Nicholas was entirely torn down and rebuilt under the Revd John Monsell in 1874. Shortly before completion, the Revd Monsell fell from the roof and was killed. The new church was consecrated in 1876. Although a great deal of change has taken place around it, the old shop nearby – already old when the current church was built – has survived.

An 1890s drawing of a building at the bottom of Mount Street. It was built in the seventeenth century and was the Wheatsheaf pub between the early 1700s and 1955, when it was finally closed. The next building up the hill was the home of George Williamson, a prolific Guildford historian and author, who created the role of Town Remembrancer – although some of his 'history' was fictional.

Still instantly recognisable, the building now serves as offices and has only seen the addition of a dormer window in the middle. The roof still retains a small amount of quaint undulation. The site of Williamson's house and garden is now another office block and car park.

Two men, seen relaxing on the Fair Field at Mount Street, c. 1870. The road behind was, until the turnpiking of Farnham Road in 1758, the main road into Guildford from the south; the very steep gradient proving perilous for the coaches using Guildford as an overnight stop. You can see the second St Nicholas' church, the tower of Holy Trinity at the top of the town in the distance, and St Mary's church to the right of centre. Above St Mary's, the site of the castle (at that time in the private ownership of Lord Grantley) is covered in dense trees. The Surrey Photo Company of 32 High Street took this image. Another photograph exists taken from the same angle at the same time, but including a third man, missing here.

The previous viewpoint still exists but is impossible to access or photograph today. Now covered with trees and bushes, it is also fenced and locked because just to the left of where the men in the earlier image sat there is a sheer drop down on the railway line, car park and the long tunnel emerging at St Catherine's. Much of Mount Street (now The Mount) has changed, but these railway cottages are the same ones visible on the right of the Victorian photograph.

The main station entrance from 1887 (but obviously taken in the mid-twentieth century). Not only does Guildford have two stations (the other is at London Road) but also after the Second World War a third was proposed, which would have been an undoubted white elephant. Parts of the structure here fell into disuse and it was totally demolished and rebuilt to modern standards in 1988.

It may have the appearance of Lego and none of the charm of the Victorian buildings, but there is still a quirky appeal to the modern structure. In 2008, the old ticket office was completely overhauled, and not only was the Travel Centre closed amidst local uproar, but numerous machines were installed to replace some of the customer service windows.

The sidings and sheds on the Guildford Park Road side of the station, taken from the Farnham Road bridge by H.C. Casserley on 15 October 1938. Visible in the top right is the new covered footbridge from the Guildford Park Road entrance, which had been built to supplement the subway the previous year when the line was electrified and the platforms were extended in length.

By chance, this train came in to the same position just as I was taking the photograph. The bridge is now difficult to see over and has a fence extending above it to prevent vandalism. Guildford Cathedral can now be seen over on Stag Hill and the mass of old Victorian sheds and sidings have been swept away with yet another modern office block and yet another car park in their place.

A touching sentiment. Here we see the widowed Mrs M. McGill in front of her house in Denzil Road in 1930. Many of the houses in this area date to the late 1800s during the building boom brought about by Guildford's rediscovered wealth from its successful local businesses and the ease with which London could be reached. Indeed, Denzil Road is only a few minutes walk from where the rear entrance to the mainline station is today. This image was used as an ersatz birthday card and Mrs McGill (who, judging by this photograph, may well have been under five feet tall) has written: 'To wish Muriel many happy returns of her birthday. Hoping she may grow up to be a good useful girl'. We don't know who Muriel is or, indeed, if she grew up to be good and useful, as the postcard was never addressed.

The same building, still in use as a single dwelling, in January 2009. All that has been lost is the original wall and Mrs McGill's railings, which probably went the way of most superfluous ironwork when it was melted down and reused as armaments in the Second World War.

4

OTHER STREETS

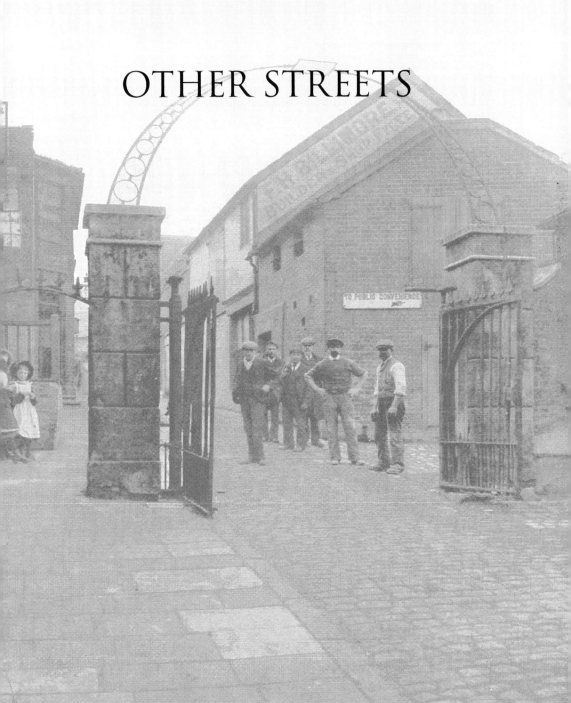

The Picture Palace, a mad collection of art nouveau ideas, on Onslow Street in the 1910s. Opened in the early 1900s, it was possibly the least comfortable of Guildford's cinemas with poorly placed pillars making some of the seats have restricted views. It changed its name to The Plaza, closed in 1957 and was then used for some years as a dance hall. After serving time as a bingo hall, it was again turned into a nightclub. On the left are the Quadrant Buildings. (Image courtesy of Simon Moulden)

This area has now been designated a Conservation Area – many would say too late. The bizarre buildings have been altered almost beyond recognition. Gone are the ornamented gables and the cupola, and a blank wall of whitewash covers the old decorations. Most of Bridge Street and this part of Onslow Street have been given over to clubs and bars. This part of Guildford changes at night. If you are under twenty-five, this might be your idea of paradise. For most other people, it is quite the opposite.

Although initially this angle may make you think you are looking out towards Onslow Street, you actually need to turn around. This is looking towards Friary Street in 1964. The Bear pub, which was sold up during that year, can just be seen in the distance on the extreme left. The building occupying most of the image behind the bus is, of course, the barracks of the 2nd Surrey Militia, built in the 1850s. The militia moved to Stoughton when the Queen's Royal West Surrey Regiment absorbed it in 1876.

The barrack buildings were demolished in 1970. The Onslow Street and Farnham Road bus stations no longer exist and Guildford's bus services now all stop at the back of the Friary Centre on Commercial Road. A taxi rank now sits at the bottom of the street and yet another featureless monolith occupies the spot of the old buildings. There is still a covered walkway down to the river, however, though it possesses none of the charm of the previous Victorian archway. In Friary Street, only the façade of the Bear remains. The rest was ripped out after the pub closed.

In this 1900s view of Haydon Place looking away from North Street you can see shops on the right which had been bought up by the Co-Operative Society, prior to their move and enlargement into the old County Hall on the corner of North Street and Leapale Road. Had you been standing here in the early nineteenth century, you would have been in Frog Lane looking ahead to the junction with Madhouse Lane!

The old cottages were swept away in the 1970s, leaving just the Live And Let Live pub further down the road (although the road after the junction was once called North Place). Until the 1980s, the right-hand side of the street served as Guildford's indoor market, although those buildings post-date the ones seen in the earlier image. In 2009, a new (and no doubt unattractive) block is being built. At least the Victorian houses further down the road remain, along with the shop on the corner.

Staff at the doorway of W.S. Slingo in Chertsey Street, the younger lady sporting a bizarre hairstyle that was fashionable in the late Edwardian era. In this wonderful image, we see the kind of shop display that belongs to a different time. Slingos were a prolific manufacturer of local postcard scenes and many of their views can be glimpsed along the top of the right-hand window.

Most Guildfordians will know the building better as Messingers, a much-loved hardware store that closed its doors for the last time in 2008. The first floor windows are unaltered, but – as is so often the case – the ground floor is unrecognisable.

Chertsey Street in the early 1900s on a postcard printed by W. Slingo, whose shop can be seen on the left – the furthest short building from the photographer. The building on the right with the two open windows is the old Dolphin Inn. It was demolished in 1915 and a new one built on the junction of Chertsey Street and North Street, itself closing in 1964. The building nearby on the left with the curious first floor window served for some years as Taplin's Guildford Sausages Ltd. The square building in the centre distance is the Ram Inn, demolished in 1913.

The left-hand side of the street is the same today, but everything else has gone. The road is now much wider at the end of the street where it joins North Street and the High Street. The building in the distance with the Doric columns was built in the 1920s and is now Guildford's Post Office. All the buildings on the right-hand side are now a faded memory. The modern building seen here is now the Slug & Lettuce pub.

Nightingale Road, *c*. 1904. This view is from next to the County High School and looking down towards Stoke Park on the right. The road here appears to be straight, but we know that at this point it bends towards the photographer. The name was changed in the 1880s; it was originally called New Road.

One hundred years on and the chap at the side of the road has changed gender. Some of the houses in the earlier view were demolished shortly after it was taken, although they were still fairly new. The replacements themselves are about a century old already. One of the only clues to show we have the right spot is the arrangement of two gables close together and a gable beneath them further down the street, as the buildings in the foreground are more recent.

Rostrevor in London Road, 13 March 1909. The house was built in 1904 and kept its original name until the 1940s, when the nearby Cross Lanes (the house of the prominent Smallpiece family) was demolished and replaced with several new buildings. From then, it adopted a number only. The sender, a Miss Bourne (who had lived in the building since its construction) writes to her sister in Worcester: 'This photo of the house has just been taken by a travelling photographer; we think it very good'.

Almost exactly 100 years on and little has changed to the house. The gates and shabby trellis have disappeared and a garage (perhaps not very necessary in 1909...) has been erected at the side. Trees have come and gone and the original porch has now been glazed. Given the alterations that often take place to houses of such size, the building has remained remarkably intact. It now faces Stoke Park and buildings used by the High School across the road.

The children's paddling pool in the recreational grounds of Stoke Park in the 1950s. The grounds were purchased for public use and to prevent building work here (oh, how times change!) by the Borough Council in 1925. It adjoins the Lido, opened in 1933 and placed for easy access from the newly constructed A3.

The pool here was rebuilt in 1989, although it clearly follows the line of the original one. It was also relined in 2002, following acts of vandalism and the lining itself coming away from the ground. We see it here in January 2009, drained and with a smattering of snow. Stoke Park mansion has been gone for over thirty years, but the Oriental shelter still stands.

A local boy sent this card of the Stoke Recreation Ground in Recreation Road, near Stoke Park, to a friend in Southampton in 1913. It seems likely that he picked this view deliberately as somewhere he spent a lot of time.

The playground is still in the same place! Distant trees made it possible to align the two shots.

The junction of Epsom Road and Albury Road on a postcard by Young's of Guildford, *c.* 1905.

Quinn's Hotel has stood on this corner for many decades. The spot is still instantly recognisable today.

Totally unrecognisable today, this is Tunsgate looking away from the High Street in the early 1900s. This gateway, by then defunct, once separated the High Street from the Borough Police Station of 1836. By the time these men (and little girls) posed between the Three Tuns pub and the public toilets, the police station had moved to North Street and the Assize Courts at the back of Tunsgate Arch had gone. The Three Tuns had originally been on the site of the later Cornmarket and this street had been its yard. (Image courtesy of Martin Leech)

Much of old Tunsgate has gone, leaving only a few buildings at the High Street end and on the Sydenham Road side. Behind the ugly 1970s shops on the right is the attractive (but sparsely populated) Tunsgate Square, featuring a popular café at its heart. It is also built on the site of the old Playhouse Arcade. On the left is the most crucial stop for any visitor to Guildford – the Tourist Information Centre.

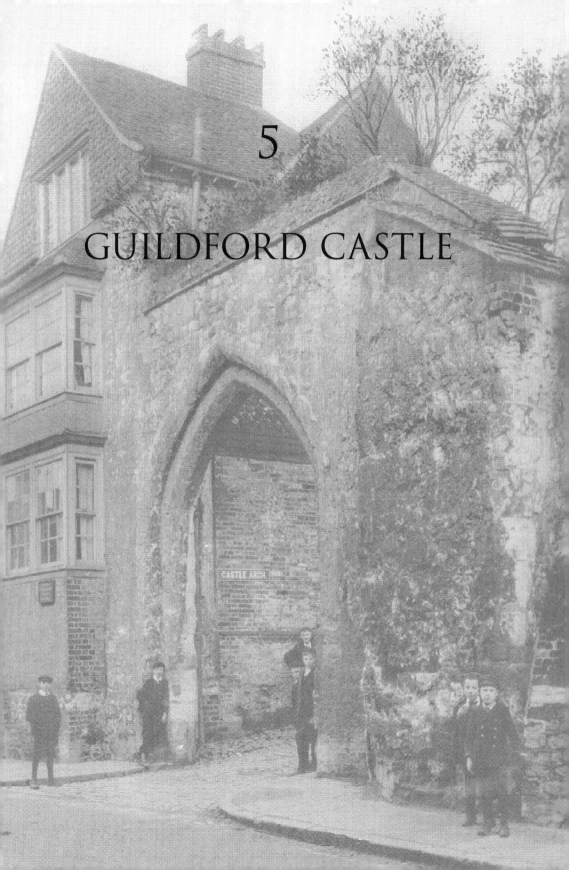

5

GUILDFORD CASTLE

A well-known image of local dignitaries at the formal opening of the Castle Grounds by the Mayor, Mr W. Swayne, and Lord Midleton on 28 June 1888. It is said it was raining heavily and the umbrellas in the hands of most of the guests prove this. This image was taken in front of the bandstand, with the photographer's back to the bowling green.

Almost exactly 116 years later, to the day. After closing for extensive renovation work, including the replacement of floors and a roof for the first time in 400 years, the Castle Keep reopened on 26 June 2004. After a procession up the High Street and speeches from the High Sheriff and Mary Alexander of Guildford Museum, the building was opened to public scrutiny. People were queuing for up to two hours to get inside. Minstrels, shown here, eased the wait by playing Medieval music.

The Castle Keep, covered in foliage (not necessarily ivy), *c.* 1890 . The keep is well hidden from Guildford shoppers, who would not know it existed if they didn't leave the High Street. Although the castle was set up shortly after the Norman Invasion, the keep dates from the early twelfth century and was built in two stages. The King initially used it as lodgings, Henry II spending the Christmas of 1154 in the building. However, by the end of the twelfth century the king was staying in more comfortable accommodation and the keep became the County Gaol for Surrey and Sussex.

In 2009, the climbing plants have gone. The keep has undergone a transformation. There have been various periods of restoration to the building including in 1914, the 1940s, the early 1950s, 1989 and 2003–4. The render on the walls now marks where the original battlements from the first stage of the building were discovered during the latest renovation work. Original lead draining chutes were found and modern versions were reinserted. The keep now contains information panels and a model of how it once appeared *c.* 1300.

Opposite above: This rare and unusual angle of the motte and castle grounds from the west was taken shortly after it was opened to the public. At the bottom left is the terracotta fountain that was installed close to the lower Castle Street entrance. Having vanished a whole century ago, many people wonder what became of it. In the late Victorian years, there were many more trees on the motte than today.

Opposite below: It is not possible to get exactly the same angle today due to the landscaping of the gardens; even this shot was taken standing right next to the wall of Castle House on top of a flowerbed. The small shelter, right of centre, still stands (although now barred and gated) and is still choked with ivy. Trees have been removed to improve the view and others have been chopped down because they had died. This can make standing on top of the motte quite windy at times. This area is now extremely popular with people taking their lunch breaks in the summer months.

Above right: Four gentlemen on and around the cannon outside the keep in the 1930s. This was a day excursion and another image shows the same group in a boat on the Wey. The cannon was captured in the Boer War and initially stood by the Tunsgate entrance to the castle grounds. In the 1910s, it was moved up to the top of the motte but it too has long since disappeared, most likely another victim of the war effort. Behind them you can just see the large brass plaque with a hugely erroneous history of the castle embossed into it.

Right: The brass plaque was later placed inside the keep, but fell down in May 1994 and then disappeared before being traced by the gardeners when the keep reopened after extensive renovations in 2004. It now sits on the ground floor of the building. A modern metal staircase leads into the original first floor entrance, following the rough line of the Medieval steps. This replaced a wooden staircase from 1990 that ran in the other direction and eventually rotted.

Looking from the bottom of the spiral staircase in the north wall towards the chapel on the first floor, *c.* 1920. The interior of the keep retained this appearance until the recent renovation works. Though replaced several times, the arrangement of gallery and staircase down to the ground floor was still used up to the time the keep closed in September 2000. The metal railings across the entrance into the chapel were still there at that time. The large arch would not have been present when the keep was in Royal use and came as part of alterations in the sixteenth century.

The same spot in 2009 gives a greater understanding in context, now a floor and ceiling have been put in place. The floor is entirely free-standing, supported by massive steel girders and posts on the ground floor. It does not touch the walls at any point. The walls have also been covered in lime mortar, similar to a mix that would have been used originally, but with some of the destructive chemicals removed.

Little from this snapshot taken from the roof of the castle keep in 1937 remains today. In the distance, cottages and whole roads in Charlotteville were pulled down in the 1960s. On the extreme left, the long-lost Tunsgate Baptist Chapel. In front of us, Candy Corner. At the bottom left, a whole terrace of cottages on Castle Street that were demolished in the 1970s.

At first glance, things don't appear to have changed so much – you can see some of the old Tunsgate shops and the buildings around the Tunsgate entrance to the castle grounds are still *in situ*. However, if they were to walk up the Castle Street and Sydenham Road of 2009, a local from 1937 would not recognise it as Guildford at all.

The War Memorial, designed by Frederick Hodgson, and unveiled in the Castle Grounds (still designated as a Garden of Remembrance) on 6 November 1921. Unlike many memorials, it has remained here ever since. A tall hedge had previously stood on this spot. In the distance you can see a wall of Tunsgate Baptist Chapel. Hundreds of the names of Guildford's dead adorn the structure.

Almost nothing has changed. The sundial has disappeared and the central monolith with the names of those killed in the Second World War did not appear until the shockingly late date of 1995. On the main memorial, two names of those subsequently found to have not been killed after all were removed in later years. The memorial is still the centre of the town's Remembrance Sunday ceremony every year.

Gardeners at work mowing the bowling green in the autumn, *c.* 1905. Without the proliferation of fertilisers and weed killers in use today, the men have done quite a good job of keeping the grass tidy. At this time it wasn't used as a bowling green at all, being given over as part of the park. Bowling, which had first taken place on this site centuries before, was reinstated in 1907.

The terraces have changed and a rather stark shelter now sits beneath the Victorian bandstand. The bowling green is now like a sheet of glass and the local bowls club uses it on an almost daily basis every summer. Many people happily sit on the benches watching them play. Bands often give Sunday concerts above, and several dramatic societies put on their productions in the upper part of the grounds in July and August.

Castle Arch, the replacement entrance to the Royal Palace, built by John of Gloucester (the King's Master Mason) in 1256 as part of a rebuilding programme. To the left of the arch can be seen a wing of the seventeenth-century mansion of Castle Arch, largely built (or extended) by the Carters. This became the base of the Surrey Archaeological Society in 1898 and about a decade later the Museum opened. A single-storey exhibition gallery was built along Quarry Street in 1911.

There have been few changes over the generations. The tiles have been removed from the arch and much of the arch itself has been reconstructed, especially when a lorry took out a large section of it in 1984, and the chalk caverns were reopened to replace the missing section with stone from the same location. The chimney has changed and the cottages that once ran up the inside of the arch have been taken over by the Museum or demolished.

6

EVENTS AND
GUILDFORD LIFE

The laying of the foundation stone of the current St Saviour's church by Mrs Randall Davidson on 14 September 1898. In 1876 a tin chapel was built in Woodbridge Road. It was replaced by an attractive red brick church in 1892 which only lasted a few years before the present church was built across the road in what had been the garden of a house called 'The Elms'. It took eight years to complete.

Although traffic now swarms around the site of St Saviour's church, it is unchanged except for the addition of a glass extension to the north. In 1906 two local men engaged in an unofficial competition to see who could scale the unfinished spire fastest. Although this is now a piece of local folklore, there sadly do not seem to be any photographs of this event.

An extremely rare image from a 3D stereoview by Hugh Langelaan of Chiddingfold, showing the destruction of the town bridge on 15 February 1900. Floodwater and timber from nearby Moon's yard (where the White House pub stands today) weakened the Medieval bridge until it collapsed, with the central pillar giving way the next day. This was taken from the bottom of the High Street looking towards Mount Street. Planking erected at the bottom of the photograph shows this was probably taken a few days later.

The new town bridge opened on 5 February 1902 and was used by traffic until the new road system was completed in the early 1970s. Since 1971, it has seen pedestrians only.

The town bridge, only four years old at this point, showing the damage sustained by the great storm of 2 August 1906. Locals crowded round all sites of damage the following day, just as they do 100 years on. Nearly all images of the damage concentrate on the more spectacular incidents here, in Woodbridge Road, Josephs Road and Shalford Road. There is little photographic record of the smaller tribulations suffered by many local householders and businesses.

The bridge might look the same now, but many will recall it was largely replaced in 1985 after being deemed unsafe. The parts of the bridge that are visible to those walking over it are original but the internal superstructure has been rebuilt.

A unique image of the tree that fell on a house in Josephs Road during the massive storm of 2 August 1906. There had been a great deal of thunder and lightning accompanied by a roaring gale. Two people were killed in Woodbridge Road and many properties were damaged. Most of the images of the aftermath were taken the following day, when it is curious to note it appeared to be fairly sunny. This particular shot was taken a few days later, by which time the tree had already been stripped of its branches and foliage.

A century on and it is still easy to recognise this site. The houses on the left are largely untouched. There are more houses on both sides of the road, particularly on the right, which was mostly empty in 1906, but virtually nothing has been demolished. The road is much wider and a few yards down from here, Josephs Road today leads out into the busy thoroughfare of Ladymead.

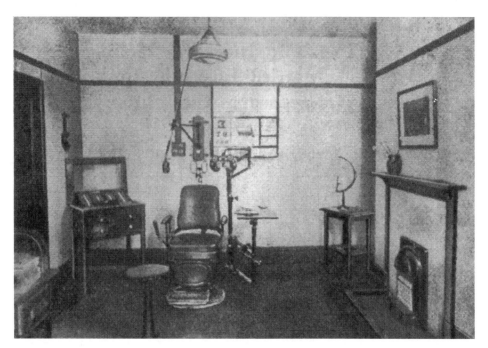

Above: One of the consulting rooms inside Horstmann's opticians next to Holy Trinity church in the High Street *c.* 1935. Mr Frederick Horstmann was originally an antique dealer and clockmaker in the Upper High Street but went on to become the town's first qualified optician and moved to this site in 1909. The advertisement here stated this room was complete with modern refracting equipment. Some Guildford residents may even recall the huge pair of 'granny glasses' that once adorned the front of the shop.

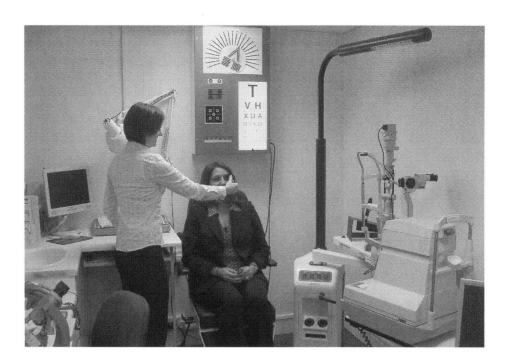

Opposite below: Bateman's bought up the business in 1983 which is in turn now controlled by Vision Express. Much has changed, and the ground floor consulting area has long since been gutted and rebuilt. Staff kindly posed for this image which shows a great deal more hardware than was available in the 1930s.

Right: An unknown Guildford street in 1907, on a privately produced photographic postcard. This is a very strange image, showing an anonymous and almost archetypal female tramp crossing a road. A well-to-do young couple in the background are smiling in her direction. It's perfectly likely this was taken in the Charlotteville area and the woman was making her way to - or from - the Casual Ward at the Spike in Warren Road. The houses might also be in one of the streets off Woodbridge Road. The sender writes 'Hope you won't go like this poor dear but look for better fish'.

When Richard Stilgoe was the County Sheriff in 1998, he said in a TV interview that Surrey could be 'an awful place to live if you're poor or if you're unemployed or if you're miserable'. Things have moved on since the earlier image was taken and the ragged tramp is largely a relic of the past. Today we are far more aware of the issue of homelessness and that it is a situation that can befall anyone who is in the wrong place at the wrong time. There are organisations who try to alleviate the problem and Guildford has at least three shelters for the homeless. A major success story in giving some people a job has, of course, been *The Big Issue*. George is one of Guildford's vendors and is usually seen at the end of Swan Lane.

For many decades, formal announcements have been made just as often from the steps of Holy Trinity church as from the balcony of the Guildhall. These days, however, you are far less likely to see a stage erected as is shown here, on the occasion of the Proclamation of George V as King on 11 May 1910. The High Sheriff, Sir Harry Waechter, surrounded by Surrey Mayors, is reading it.

In many ways, you might have to do a double take to ensure you're not seeing an image from the same period. However, this is 10 May 2007 and the Mayor, Mike Nevins, is posing for the press in the company of appropriately attired employees of Guildford Borough Council (including the author – obviously not seen here) and children from nearby Sandfield Primary School. The event was the long-awaited reopening of the fishpond in the Castle Grounds, fully restored after having shrunk over the years and finally being filled in. The lion apparently came from White Lion Walk but conversations with it did not elicit any reply!

The centre of Guildford seems to witness a major fire every ten years on average, though a century ago this was more frequent. At the time, this was the biggest fire Guildford had seen for many years, although Reeks' would burn down the following year and Gates' the year after that. White's draper's store in the High Street (where Marks & Spencer stands today) was partially destroyed on the afternoon of 24 June 1914. This card was sent three weeks later from a member of the famous local Crookes family. Part of it reads 'A heap of burned shirts in the corner, the floor was all glass to walk on. Not quite everything destroyed in this room, but it will all have to be rebuilt'. White's opened in Guildford in 1877 and was taken over by Marks & Spencer in 1962.

At the time of writing, this was the most recent serious fire in the town centre. The only recent fire before this was the destruction of the old Robert Dyas store in the middle of the High Street in 2001. Here, we see the roof of Somerset House alight on 19 December 2006. Repairs to the building were slow and scaffolding surrounded the site subsequently for many months. (Photograph by Alice Fage)

By the Stoke Hotel in the 1920s, a local bobby poses with a cyclist (possibly making a delivery) in the rain.

Policing in 2008 – and a bit noisier. Two members of the Surrey Constabulary working outside one of the music stages at Guilfest in Stoke Park. The festival has a reputation for being one of the safest and friendliest music events anywhere in the country and is frequented by families and people of all ages. Arrests are rare and almost always drug or drink related. Guilfest organiser Tony Scott has become a local legend through his work, although it must be said that some nearby residents understandably do not look forward to a weekend in early July every year.

Night events in Guildford stretch way back into history. It could be said that the infamous Guy Riots of the 1850s were such a thing. This curious image shows a safer nocturnal occasion. This deceptively flimsy windmill was erected at Mount Farm as part of the celebrations for the Coronation of King George VI on 12 May 1937 and had rotating sails. Chaplin's newsagents of North Street sold this souvenir photograph.

Now an event gleefully awaited by thousands of townsfolk every year, we see the view in the High Street of torch bearers ready to process towards Stoke Park where a fairground and firework display await. It is arranged by Guildford Lions, who rely on donations from the public to stage this superb event. This image dates from 5 November 2008. It is a shame you cannot hear the constant Python-esque cries of 'Burn the witch!' – a line which never seems to lose its novelty.

Instantly recognisable as a dramatic scene from the 1968 flood. It began with a heavy downpour on 14 September and quickly swamped the lowest parts of the town. It reached a height of six feet in places and hundreds of thousands of pounds of damage resulted. A tasteful plaque on the side of St Nicolas' church today shows the water level.

Although the 1968 flood has not been matched in living memory, the Wey still floods frequently although such extensive damage to buildings these days is rare. Because so much of the land around parts of the river are on the same low level, when it does breach its banks it can have spectacular results. Here is the area of Millmead and Millmead Lock totally submerged in the floods of January 2008. The water level only lasted for a day before draining away. (Photograph by Simon Harvey-Williams)

The Horse & Groom pub at the top of North Street. It started life as a barn, built by John Child, in 1690. It was a pub by 1811 and the elevation facing North Street dates from 1874. However, it is for this event – the Guildford Pub Bombings of 5 October 1974 – that the building will always be remembered. Five people were killed and dozens injured by an IRA bomb. The pub was marked for attack because off-duty soldiers from nearby Aldershot used it.

Although the pub recovered from this dark episode, it shut its doors for commercial reasons in 1992 and is now used as a furniture showroom, with only the section partially destroyed by the bomb being externally remodelled.

The Pranksters Theatre Company was formed in 1977 and took its name from a radical 1960s organisation in America. This production of *Look Back In Anger* was performed in 1981 at the Bellerby Theatre and shows Kate Webb (still a member over quarter of a century later), Stephen Chudley and Hamish McLean. The Bellerby Theatre has now been superseded by productions at The Electric Theatre and The Mill Studio Theatre and is seldom used except by the Guildford Conservatoire. Its days are said to be numbered. (Photograph by Jennifer Haynes)

The party scene from *Romeo & Juliet*, as presented by Pranksters around Guildford High Street in July 2008. Performed in modern dress, the choreographed fights in front of the Guildhall actually caused some passers-by to phone the police during the dress rehearsal, fearing they were witnessing knife attacks. This happier moment was taken under Tunsgate Arch and shows Nathan Jones, Anne Leggett, Geoff Trowell and Graeme Aston. (Photograph by Peter Sillick)

7

LOST GUILDFORD

From an advertisement for the Alexandra Laundry on the junction of Harvey Road and Baillie Road *c.* 1925. In an era before there were many household appliances, Guildford had several buildings such as this one. Positioned, as it was, right next to St Luke's Hospital in Warren Road it must have had a constant supply of work. At the time the photograph was taken, the laundry claimed to be 'the newest and most modern laundry in the District'.

The hill is not so steep today – if it ever was that steep in the first place – and now the east side of the street is full of modern houses.

Opposite above: Guildford Odeon as seen from Epsom Road in the 1950s. The cinema was opened to the public on 13 May 1935, with a showing of *Brewster's Millions*. In the 1960s it also held concerts by such popular acts as The Beatles, The Rolling Stones and Cliff Richard. Most Guildfordians have fond memories of the building.

A cautionary tale – never trust property developers. When the old Odeon was demolished in 2002, promises were made that at least part of the impressive portico would be preserved and left *in situ* as the new exclusive housing development of Trinity Gate rose up around it. Of course, this didn't happen and, with the exception of some delightful film quotes running across the pavement on the High Street side, there is nothing left to remind you of this much-loved building.

Allen House in the early 1950s. It was built by Thomas Cranfield around 1660 and was for many years used by the Royal Grammar School. Dr Richard Christophers remembers the building from when he was a student there in the late 1940s. He recalls it was a fine building in a state of dilapidation, with rotten boards and staircases and freezing cold in the winter. He also recalls several rooms in the basement used as dens and the discovery of a canoe in a short underground tunnel that one of the masters attempted to repair.

The structure came down in 1964 during extensive renovation of the north side of the Upper High Street. A much-needed and much larger modern set of buildings for the Royal Grammar School was built in its place and the site of the house is now an open space at the front of the grounds. All that remains of the site is the public park behind the site leading towards York Road car park.

Opposite above: Massey's chemist shop on the junction of North Street and Upper High Street in 1948. The company also owned a second shop at the other end of the street next to the town bridge. It is seen here nicely whitewashed, which had been done fairly recently on the brickwork. To the right you can see the edge of Constitutional Hall which many people will remember was the home of the much-loved Thorp booksellers.

All that is left from the previous view is Constitutional Hall. Everything else was swept away in the 1960s, although the buildings running away from the corner were only supposed to be temporary. Thorp's closed for good some years ago in spite of a massive struggle to survive the wave of Internet purchasing. Since then, several businesses have used the large old building for short-term lets and it is, at the time of writing, unoccupied. The statue of Guildford's most famous son, George Abbot, was placed here in 1993, close to his burial place.

The Midland Bank, built next to Constitutional Hall by Whinney, Son & Austen Hall in the 1920s. Facing the larger edifice of Barclays Bank over the street, it at least ensured it had a larger door. This image was taken from an architectural magazine of 1927.

Not surprisingly, the current building dates from the mid-1970s. The Midland Bank moved out of the site in early 2008 and, at the time of writing, it is empty.

The Tunsgate Baptist Chapel in the early 1900s. Often popping up in the background of postcards of the Castle Grounds, actual direct views of the chapel are fairly scarce. It was built in 1860 and largely remodelled in 1874, when it also gained different windows. The chapel also had its own burial ground and when it was demolished in 1954 the bones that were unearthed were reburied in The Mount cemetery. There were reports of ghost sightings around this time. (Image courtesy of Simon Moulden)

After the chapel came down, the area was an open car park for eighteen years until Tunsgate Square was built in 1972, on the 700th anniversary of the Ascension of Edward I. Tunsgate is now much wider and the first two buildings on the right in the previous view have been demolished to make the passage of traffic easier into Sydenham Road.

The Borough Hall (shown here in the early 1900s) was built from local Bargate stone on the corner of North Street and Leapale Road in 1861. The County Assizes were held here and it also housed the town Post Office from 1870. In 1912, it became the Theatre Royal and underwent external alterations (losing the attractive gables, which were filled in). The theatre shut after twenty years but reopened as Guildford's repertory theatre in 1946 with the Co-Op next door. A fire destroyed the theatre in April 1963. It was finally demolished as late as 1984, outlasting Peak's buildings further down the street by two decades. (Image courtesy of Simon Moulden)

Ugly, formulaic, functional, modern and yet already outdated – the replacement was for some years the home of Index, who were themselves bought out by Argos. The curious thing here is that Argos has another branch less than five minutes walk up the road on the Upper High Street.

Without doubt, the most famous of Guildford's many breweries and instantly recognisable. The Friary brewery was built on the site of the former Dominican Friary founded by Eleanor of Provence in 1275. Before the brewery, the land was used as barracks. The brewery began under Thomas Taunton and Charles Hoskins Master, *c.* 1865. The photograph here probably dates to 1970. The brewery has already closed, but traffic lights have not yet been erected at the Bridge Street and Onslow Street junction. (Image courtesy of Peter Williams)

After the brewery closed in 1969, the buildings came down piece by piece from 1973. The tower was finally brought down in February 1974, after which the site was cleared and remained vacant for some years. Before building work on the Friary Centre began, archaeologists discovered extensive remains of the Friary foundations and dozens of burials (which were reinterred in St Mary's in 1987). A roof garden, water feature, decent town square and partial preservation of the remains were promised – and all those promises were broken.

The Guildford Sports Centre (shown here *c.* 1980) was constructed on land next to the River Wey at the back of the old cattle market site and opened in 1972. A large, square building, it not only housed a popular swimming pool but also had facilities for badminton, cricket, athletics, netball and squash. It was the first phase of the redevelopment of the area. In the background is the Bedford Road car park, built shortly afterwards.

In 1993 The Spectrum Leisure Centre on Parkway superseded the Sports Centre, just outside the town. At the same time, it was decided to replace the old building with a new multiplex Odeon cinema on roughly the same footprint. Adjoining this on the same plot is the Old Orleans pub.

The cattle market was held in the High Street until 1865, decamped to North Street, and was moved to a larger, dedicated site on Woodbridge Road in 1896. It remained until 1976, when it found a new home at Slyfield, until it shut for good in 2000. This image across the holding pens, looking towards St Saviour's church, dates from *c.* 1910.

Just the tip of the spire of the church can be seen today. The whole area was cleared in the early 1970s, removing not only the cattle market but also Guildford's huge gasholders. On the site was built the Sports Centre, Bedford Road multi-storey car park, the new police station and – dating from the same period and shown here – the Law Courts.

The very essence of 'Lost Guildford', where Park Street joins Farnham Road as it looked in the 1930s. It is well known that the cottages were pulled down in 1957 and were by that time condemned as unfit for human habitation. There can be few people who would not wish they still existed. Park Street was extremely narrow and was met by a one-way system cutting through what is now part of the car park by the George Abbot pub.

The last part of the old road was lost in the 1970s. It is now an extremely busy multi-lane road leading to the station, the Hog's Back, the town centre and beyond. Needless to say, the author took a big risk by standing in the middle of the road to quickly snap this!

The Connaught Hotel *c.* 1940, shortly before it was demolished. The Queen Anne style building had originally been called Guildford House and had been the home of the Crookes family, one of the largest and most successful of the Guildford breweries (which was behind). It is ironic that in its final years it served as a temperance hotel. Situated right next to the River Wey at its most vulnerable point, it flooded frequently.

The demolition of the hotel led to the construction of the Farnham Road bus station. Where once stood a fine old building, we now have a line of recycling bins.

The original Jolly Farmer pub *c.* 1900, just beyond the end of Quarry Street on the road heading to Shalford. It is not known when the pub first started trading but it is thought to have been in the early 1800s. An opening at the side led to Charles Leroy's boathouse just behind the pub. (Image courtesy of Peter Williams)

The Jolly Farmer was rebuilt in this much more pleasing style in 1913. It is one of few structures in the vicinity that was not swept away in the massive road building project in the 1960s and 1970s. The pub has also undergone a name change to The Weyside.

Woolworth was built on the site of the old Lion Hotel in 1957, and they retained the statue from the old structure (unsurprisingly named Leo by the builders). This image by W. Dennett of Guildford shows some of the staff in a Woolworth's company magazine of 1958, which had a feature on the new Guildford store. The manager, Mr Fitzpatrick, sits in the centre. This store was itself demolished in 1984 to make way for the arcade of White Lion Walk. The original lion sadly bit the dust at the same time and the one seen today is a replica.

Both past and present are lost. A century-old institution, once beloved of the nation but now left behind in the marketplace, the company shut its doors forever at the end of December 2008. This shot of the final store in Friary Street, amidst great building improvements taking place, was taken just days before the company went out of business (even selling off the shop fittings). However, a final glimmer of hope; at the time of writing it was rumoured that the company name was about to be relaunched as an online retailer.

Other titles published by The History Press

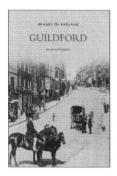

Guildford (Images of England)
PHILIP HUTCHINSON

Saxon Guildford grew up around the area of the current St Mary's church and a Norman castle was founded in the town shortly after 1066. The town developed in Medieval times as it became rich through the woollen trade. This fascinating book depicting Guildford's past is illustrated with over 200 absorbing images and will provide a nostalgic journey to those who have always lived in the town and to newcomers interested in learning more about the area's history.

978 0 7509 4203 7

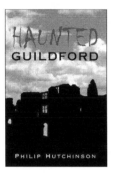

Haunted Guildford
PHILIP HUTCHINSON

From heart-stopping accounts of apparitions, manifestations and related supernatural phenomena to first-hand encounters with ghouls and spirits, this collection of stories contains new and well-known spooky tales from around Guildford. Drawing on historical and contemporary sources, *Haunted Guildford* contains a chilling range of ghostly accounts that is sure to appeal to anyone interested in the supernatural history of the area.

978 0 7524 3826 9

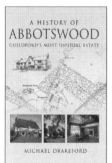

A History of Abbotswood: Guildford's Most Unusual Estate
MICHAEL DRAKEFORD

Abbotswood is a favoured suburb in Guilford. This book explores the very best of suburban architecture, and in doing so provides the strongest possible argument for its retention. The book will fascinate those interested in Guildford's local history, but will also appeal to anyone with a broader interest in the period, and in particular the Arts and Crafts style as well as those hoping to replicate the characteristic and distinctive architecture of the period.

978 1 86077 521 5

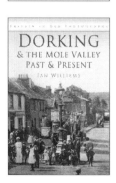

Dorking & the Mole Valley Past & Present
IAN WILLIAMS

Dorking, the commercial centre of the Mole Valley, lies equidistant between London and the south coast. Surrounding the historic town, the valley is an area of outstanding beauty. Featured here are fascinating images of the villages of Brockham, Betchworth, Buckland, Leigh, Newdigate, Capel, Ockley, Beare Green, The Holmwoods, Holmbury, Abinger, Wotton, Westcott, Leith Hill and Mickleham. Here we discover how much the area has changed by comparing old postcards with modern photographs of the same view.

978 0 7509 4582 0

Visit our website and discover thousands of other History Press books.
www.thehistorypress.co.uk

Printed in Great Britain
by Amazon